discover countries

Norway

Elaine Jackson

WAYLAND

Published in paperback in 2014 by Wayland
Copyright Wayland 2014

Wayland
Hachette Children's Books
338 Euston Road
London NW1 3BH

Wayland Australia
Level 17/207 Kent Street,
Sydney, NSW 2000

Concept design: Jason Billin
Editors: Nicola Edwards and Kelly Davis
Designer: Amy Sparks

Produced for Wayland by
White-Thomson Publishing Ltd

www.wtpub.co.uk
+44 (0) 0843 2087 460

British Library Cataloguing in Publication Data

Jackson, Elaine, 1954
Norway. – (Discover countries)
1. Norway – Juvenile literature
I. Title II. Series   948.1'05-dc22

ISBN-13: 978 0 7502 8091 4

Printed in China
2 4 6 8 10 9 7 5 3 1
Wayland is a division of Hachette Children's Books
an Hachette UK company
www.hachette.co.uk

All data in this book was researched in 2010
and has been collected from the latest sources available at that time.

Picture credits
1, Dreamstime/Natalia Rumyantseva; 3 (top), Shutterstock/Albert H. Teich; 3 (bottom), Dreamstime/Alvov; 4 (map), Stefan Chabluk;
5, Dreamstime/Tyler Olson; 6, Dreamstime/Iryna Sosnytska; 7, Dreamstime/Jardach; 8, istockphoto/Andrey Artykov;
9, Alamy/Anna Yu; 10, Dreamstime/Serban Enache; 11, Dreamstime/Natalia Rumyantseva; 12, istockphoto/Ekely; 13, Alamy/Art Kowalsky;
14, Shutterstock/Albert H. Teich; 15, Alamy/Bryan and Cherry Alexander; 16, Alamy/Niall Benvie; 17, Alamy/Danita Delimont;
18, Alamy/Edward Parker; 19, Dreamstime/Alis Gheorghe Leonte; 20, Dreamstime/Alvov; 21, Shutterstock/Bent G. Nordeng;
22, Dreamstime/Martinmark; 23, Dreamstime/Somatuscan; 24, Shutterstock/Lelde; 25, Alamy/David Robertson;
26, Shutterstock/Zbynek Burival; 27, Getty Images/Geir Olsen/AFP; 28, Shutterstock/Witold Kaszkin;
29, Dreamstime/Eleonoracerna; cover (right) Dreamstime/Serban Enache cover (left) Shutterstock/Tyler Olson

Contents

Discovering Norway

Norway, bordered to the west by the Atlantic Ocean, covers the western part of Scandinavia and is the most northern country in Europe. It is long, narrow and mountainous, with nearly one-third of the country lying north of the Arctic Circle.

Norway's rugged coastline is broken by huge fjords (long, narrow coastal valleys with steep sides) and thousands of islands, such as the Lofoten Islands, the Svalbard archipelago and Jan Mayen. With a population of only five million, it is one of the most sparsely populated countries in Europe.

Norway statistics

Area: 323,802 sq km (125,020 sq miles)

Capital city: Oslo

Government type: Constitutional monarchy

Bordering countries: Finland, Sweden, Russia

Currency: Norwegian krone (NOK)

Language: Bokmal Norwegian (official), Nynorsk Norwegian (official), small Sami- and Finnish-speaking minorities; note – Sami is official in six municipalities

🔺 This map shows Norway's main cities, bordering countries, coastline and islands.

Sailors and warriors

Norway's greatest impact on history was during the Viking Age (800–1100 CE). The Vikings, who were great sailors and warriors, left Norway and travelled to other countries, such as Britain, Ireland, Iceland and Greenland. Some went to raid and steal, while others settled in the new lands as farmers and traders. The Vikings, led by Leif Ericson, son of the Norwegian Viking Erik the Red, founded a settlement in North America almost 500 years before Columbus 'discovered' the New World.

At various times in history, Norway was part of Denmark and Sweden, finally becoming independent again in 1905. Norway stayed neutral during the world wars and was a founding member of the United Nations in 1945.

Kings and prime ministers

Norway has a royal family and a parliament. The king and his family have no real political power, their role being mainly ceremonial. Norway's elected parliament, the Storting, passes laws and decides how the national income should be spent. The Storting is elected every four years and is led by the prime minister.

► Ferryboat services are indispensable, for both locals and tourists, to access settlements such as Flam (shown here), deep in the fjords, on the western side of Norway.

Landscape and climate

Two-thirds of Norway is covered by mountains, and much of the landscape was shaped during the Ice Age. Fjords were cut into the land by glaciers and flooded by the sea when the Ice Age ended. Today, there are still more than 1,500 glaciers in Norway, including Jostedalsbreen which, at 487 sq km (188 sq miles), is the largest glacier in Europe.

Contrasting landscapes

Norway can be divided into four geographical areas. In northern Norway, the landscape is a mixture of mountains and valleys. In south-east Norway there are large areas of forest, gentle valleys and rich arable land. The landscape in the south-west is very dramatic, with high plateaux, steep valleys and deep fjords. The Sognefjord, Norway's longest and deepest fjord, and Galdhøpiggen, Norway's highest mountain, are located here. In the central region the mountains are less steep.

Facts at a glance

Water area: 19,520 sq km (7,537 sq miles)

Highest point: Galdhøpiggen 2,469 m (8,100 ft)

Lowest point: Norwegian Sea 0 m (0 ft)

Longest river: Glomma River 130 km (80 miles)

Land area: 304,282 sq km (117,484 sq miles)

🔻 In the west of Norway, many rivers cascade down steep slopes, creating spectacular waterfalls, such as the Seven Sisters waterfall.

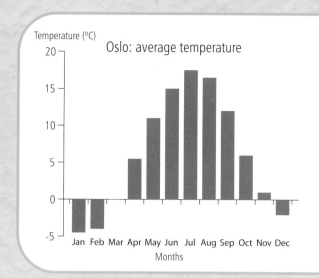

Temperature (°C)

Oslo: average temperature

Months: Jan Feb Mar Apr May Jun Jul Aug Sep Oct Nov Dec

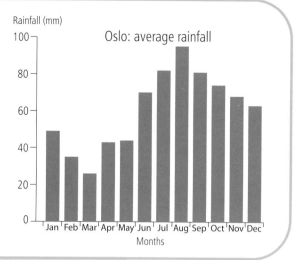

Rainfall (mm)

Oslo: average rainfall

Months: Jan Feb Mar Apr May Jun Jul Aug Sep Oct Nov Dec

A cold climate

Norway lies at about the same latitude as Alaska and northern Russia, but it is warmed by the waters of the North Atlantic Drift. Coastal areas remain mild in winter, fjords never freeze and harbours remain free of ice. However, upland areas in central Norway and areas north of the Arctic Circle experience much colder conditions. Winters are long and dark and snowfall can be heavy, making daily life difficult. Precipitation is heaviest along the west coast and on windward mountain slopes.

Land of the Midnight Sun

Norway is known as 'the Land of the Midnight Sun' because, in areas north of the Arctic Circle, during summer the sky remains light throughout day and night. In the winter, the sun never rises and there is constant night. Many people become very irritable in the summer, as they find it difficult to sleep, while in the darkness of winter, many feel gloomy and low.

▶ Tourists flock to North Cape (Nordkapp), the most northerly point in Europe, where the midnight sun can be seen from mid-May to mid-July.

DID YOU KNOW?
North of the Arctic Circle, the Northern Lights, or Aurora Borealis, caused by electrical particles colliding, fill the winter sky with displays of light and colour.

Population and health

Norway is officially the best place in the world to live, according to the United Nations Human Development Index, based on life expectancy, education and standard of living. Norwegians enjoy good childcare, excellent schools and universities, a well-developed, free health service and generous welfare systems. People who are working pay high taxes to fund these services.

A changing and ageing population

Norway's population has grown from just under 1 million in 1822 to 5 million today. Forecasts show that the population will grow to nearly 6 million by 2050.

Health and life expectancy have improved, particularly over the last 20 years, due to progress in medical care and improvements in living conditions. As life expectancy increases, the number of people aged 65 and over will increase fast, from 16.4 per cent of the population in 2013 to an estimated 22 per cent in 2050, requiring more to be spent on healthcare services for the elderly.

> **Facts at a glance**
>
> **Total population:**
>   5 million
>
> **Life expectancy at birth:**
>   80 years
>
> **Children dying before the age of five:** 0.4%
>
> **Ethnic composition:**
>   Norwegian 94.4% (includes Sami, about 60,000), other European 3.6%, other 2%

▶ According to Save the Children, Norway is the best country in which to have children because Norwegian women have access to good healthcare and generous maternity leave.

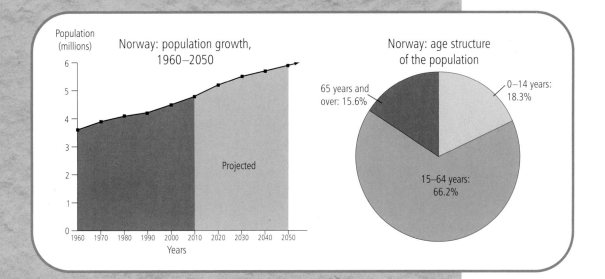

Population (millions)

Norway: population growth, 1960–2050

Projected

Years

Norway: age structure of the population

65 years and over: 15.6%

0–14 years: 18.3%

15–64 years: 66.2%

As more Norwegians get older, the types of illnesses are changing. Age is an important risk factor for heart problems, cancer and dementia (a disease of the brain). Other health problems that Norway is working to reduce in the population as a whole include muscular diseases, mental illnesses including anxiety and depression, alcoholism and drug abuse.

Sami

The Norwegian Sami are indigenous people who live far above the Arctic Circle. Sami have traditionally survived by hunting and fishing, and by herding reindeer. Reindeer are kept for their meat and skins, and also milk, which is mainly made into cheese.

DID YOU KNOW? In the past, the Sami were called 'Lapps', but this term is offensive to Sami, as it means 'a patch of cloth for mending', and suggests they wear patched clothes.

In the past, reindeer were also the main form of transport. Nowadays, reindeer sledges have largely been replaced by snowmobiles and four-wheel drive vehicles, and fewer than 10 per cent of Sami are involved in reindeer herding. The rest follow a wide range of careers including banking and teaching.

⬣ Some Sami, like this boy in his blue tunic with bands of bright red, orange and yellow, still wear traditional clothes.

Settlements and living

Norway is one of the most sparsely populated countries in Europe. Over the last 50 years, many people have moved away from remote northern and rural areas. Today most Norwegians live in small urban settlements.

Small cities and towns

Compared to most other countries, there are no really big cities in Norway. Only five settlements, Oslo, Bergen, Stavanger, Trondheim and Fredrikstad/Sarpsborg, have more than 100,000 inhabitants. About one-third of the country's population live in these five urban settlements. Of the other 914 urban settlements, only 90 have 5,000 residents or more.

Facts at a glance

Urban population:
80% (4 million)
Rural population:
20% (1 million)
Population of largest city:
875,000 (Oslo)

▼ The colourful timber-frame houses of Bryggen, the dock area of Bergen, are protected and part of a UNESCO World Heritage Site.

The main cities

Oslo, with fewer than 900,000 inhabitants, is Norway's capital and the country's main commercial, industrial and cultural centre. Bergen, a major seaport on the west coast known for shipping and fishing, is Norway's second-largest city. In 2000, Bergen was named a European City of Culture, contributing to highlighting the richness and diversity of cultures across Europe. Trondheim is the oldest city in Norway, while Stavanger is known as the 'Oil Capital of Norway'. Tromso, often called 'the Gateway to the Arctic', is a lively city, centrally located among northern Norway's snow-capped mountains.

Colourful houses

Most Norwegian houses are built of wood, with slate or corrugated-iron roofing. The houses are often painted in white or in strong, warm colours such as red or yellow. Traditionally, houses have small rooms, to keep in the warmth, and steep roofs to help the snow slide off. Windows are also small, so heat isn't lost through the glass. There is usually a wood-burning stove in the centre of the house to warm up all the rooms during the cold winters.

In rural Norway many people still live in old farmhouses in remote areas, or fishermen's cottages close to the seashore. As cities grow, more people are choosing to live in spacious urban apartments and studios.

⬥ Oslo, the Norwegian capital, is situated at the head of Oslo fjord and is the oldest of the Scandinavian capitals.

DID YOU KNOW?
Skarsvåg, the world's northernmost fishing village, is on the bleak, barren island of Magerøya. Cod caught here makes top-quality salted fish, which is then exported.

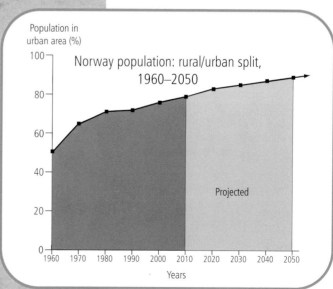

Population in urban area (%)

Norway population: rural/urban split, 1960–2050

Projected

Years

Family life

Norwegian families make frequent trips to visit relatives, as well as attending special events such as weddings, christenings, confirmations and funerals. Many Norwegian families have small cottages along the coast or in the mountains for family weekend trips.

Changing families

Although most families are made up of a mother and father and up to two children, with both parents sharing the responsibility for bringing up their children, the divorce rate has been rising.

Facts at a glance

Average children per childbearing woman:
1.8 children

Average household size:
2.2 people

⬇ Many Norwegians enjoy spending their leisure time in their family cabins, tucked away in the wilderness and surrounded by the unspoilt mountain landscape.

This has led to more children spending a lot of their childhood with only one parent, although both parents usually stay in contact with the children. Stepfamilies are the fastest-growing type of family in Norway.

Traditional weddings

Norwegians are waiting longer before marrying, the average age for a groom now being almost 36 years old and a bride 32. A hundred years ago, the average age for men was about 30 and for women was 26.

The bride often wears a white or silver wedding dress with a silver and gold crown. Dangling around the crown are small spoon-shaped bangles. These make a metallic musical sound which traditionally was thought to scare away evil spirits.

The groom wears a suit called a *bundas*. The *bundas* is covered with intricate and colourful designs; each design is unique to the district of Norway the groom comes from and makes him resemble a Norwegian prince from the past.

The couple exchange wedding rings, symbolising never-ending love. Traditionally, two small fir trees are planted on either side of the door to the couple's home as a symbol of the children to come.

▶ A wedding party outside Urnes stave church (*stavkirke*) in western Norway. The wooden church was built during the 12th and 13th centuries and is the oldest in the country.

Religion and beliefs

Most Norwegians are Christians and belong to the Evangelical Lutheran Church of Norway. Although only 3 per cent attend regular church services, many Norwegians take part in Christian festivals, such as Christmas and Easter. The largest non-Christian religion in Norway is Islam.

Folklore and myths

Norwegian folklore is rich in tales about trolls, giants, elves and gnomes. Trolls are said to live in forests and mountains, and are usually described as being ugly, mean and quarrelsome.

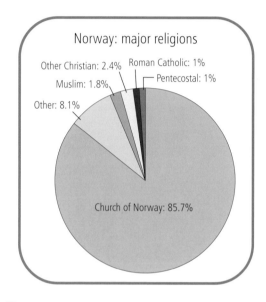

Norway: major religions

Other Christian: 2.4%
Roman Catholic: 1%
Muslim: 1.8%
Pentecostal: 1%
Other: 8.1%
Church of Norway: 85.7%

⬤ Each year, on May 17, Norwegians march through the streets, waving flags to celebrate Norway's National Day.

Norwegian folk stories about trolls include the well-known tale, 'The Three Billy Goats Gruff', in which the goats had to overcome a fierce troll who lived under a bridge.

Easter

Easter Sunday, with its message of new life, is the high point of the Christian year and many Norwegians attend church services. In the past, people have climbed mountains on Easter Sunday, to watch the sunrise, as they believed the sun danced with joy for the resurrection of Jesus. This may have started the Norwegian custom of 'going up the mountains' to their cabins at Eastertime. Traditionally, the chicken and egg are symbols of Easter in Norway, joined more recently by the chocolate-bearing Easter bunny.

During the Easter holiday, many Sami enjoy attending reindeer sledge races and taking part in *yoik* singing (traditional chanting).

Christmas traditions

At Christmas, friends and family come together to share much-loved customs. On Christmas Eve, the Christmas gnome (a jolly fellow with red stockings, a cap and long, white beard) brings presents to all the good children. In rural areas, there is a tradition called *Julebukk*. Children and adults, dressed up in costumes, led by someone dressed up as a *bukk* (a billy goat), go from house to house singing Christmas carols in exchange for treats.

Every year, the Norwegians donate a giant Christmas tree to stand in Trafalgar Square in London as a gesture of goodwill in return for the help Norway received during the Second World War.

DID YOU KNOW? An unusual national Easter pastime is reading detective stories. Newspapers and TV stations run series based on the works of famous crime novelists. Crime stories are even printed on milk cartons.

Education and learning

The Norwegian education system is one of the best in the world. All children have an equal right to education, regardless of where they live, or their gender or social and cultural background. Norway spends a lot on education and all public education is free, but parents pay fees for places at kindergartens.

Outdoor kindergartens

Today most Norwegian children attend kindergarten before they start school. Kindergartens have increased because so many mothers work and there are growing numbers of single-parent families. In 2013, 87 per cent of Norwegian children aged 1–5 attended kindergartens.

◉ A Norwegian girl looks out of a cabin in the woods, at a *naturbarnehage* (nature nursery), where learning outdoors helps children develop their curiosity and creativity.

In around 10 per cent of the kindergartens, all play and learning takes place outside. As children learn by doing, educationalists and parents believe this makes the children tougher and also more creative and independent.

Facts at a glance

Children in primary school:
Male 98%, Female 98%
Children in secondary school:
Male 96%, Female 97%
Literacy rate (over 15 years):
100%

At school

Education in Norway is compulsory for all children aged 6 to 16. The school system is divided into three parts: elementary school (age 6–13); lower secondary school (13–16); and upper secondary school (16–19).

For the first few years, the school day lasts about four hours, but it increases gradually to six or seven hours. Children have one main teacher throughout elementary school. Class size is regulated by law. In primary school, the maximum class size is 28, and for the lower secondary school it is 30. However, the average class size is much lower than these limits. All textbooks and notebooks are provided free of charge in elementary and lower secondary schools. School cafeterias are rare, so most children bring packed lunches to school.

A school visit to Vigeland Sculpture Park in Oslo. Norwegian schools are very informal. School uniforms are completely unknown and teachers are addressed by their first names.

From school to university

Higher education plays an important role. In 2013, 32 per cent of 19 to 24-year-olds were in higher education. Young people study academic degrees at universities, or go to colleges to gain qualifications related to specific jobs, such as teaching, engineering, social work and healthcare.

DID YOU KNOW?
Schoolchildren often take part in 'school patrols'. Trained by the police and wearing easily recognisable uniforms, they ensure that motorists stop at pedestrian crossings for children on their way to school.

Employment and economy

Norway was once mainly a country of farmers, fishermen, foresters and sailors. Today, Norway is a highly developed, industrial country with a well-educated workforce. Most employment is in service industries and manufacturing.

A prosperous economy

Norway has many natural resources, which have helped make it one of the world's most prosperous countries. Although economic growth has declined recently, Norway has fared much better during the international financial crisis that began in 2008 than many other industrialised countries, because of its strong, modern economy.

Facts at a glance

Contributions to GDP:
agriculture: 3%
industry: 41%
services: 56%

Labour force:
agriculture: 3%
industry: 21%
services: 76%

Female labour force:
47% of total

Unemployment rate:
3.1%

⬆ Large forests of Norway spruce produce vast quantities of timber for pulp, to be used in the paper industry.

The oil industry

Towards the end of the twentieth century, the oil industry had become the leading branch of Norway's economy, closely followed by finance. Oil was first extracted from Norwegian-controlled areas of the North Sea in 1966.

Many other jobs depend on the oil industry, including those involving the construction of oil-drilling platforms, the manufacture of equipment and the provision of supplies and services. Natural gas is present in the same area as oil, and most of it is also exported.

Oil and gas will continue to play a leading role in Norway's economy over the next few decades, meeting Norway's own energy needs as well being major export commodities, although they will gradually get less important as the deposits are used up.

Knowing that oil and gas production will eventually decline, the Norwegian government saves almost all the money it makes from the oil sector and invests it for the future benefit of the country's citizens.

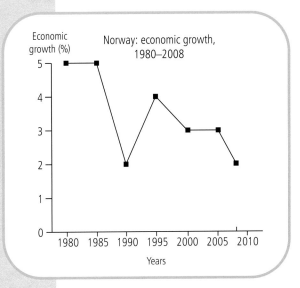

Norway: economic growth, 1980–2008

DID YOU KNOW?
Norwegians have twice voted not to join the European Union (EU). Many Norwegians are concerned about being allowed to maintain small-scale farming and fishing.

An oil rig in a Norwegian fjord. Oil and gas make up nearly half of exports and over 30 per cent of state revenue.

19

Industry and trade

Besides oil, the other major industries on which Norway relies are fishing, pulp and paper, forestry, mining, manufacturing, such as chemical and metal products, and shipping. The country relies on exports, as its population and home markets are small, and Norway is situated close to the major markets of Europe. Norway's main exports are oil and petroleum products, metals and fish.

The fishing industry

Norway has a long history as a fishing nation, and fishing plays a central part in life and culture along the coast. As Norway controls some of the world's richest fishing grounds in the North Sea, fishing is one of its major export industries. However, Norway also faces the problem of how to avoid depleting fish stocks while maintaining a profitable industry.

The fishing industry includes traditional fishing and deep-sea fishing by modern trawlers, aquaculture (fish farming) and processing of all kinds of seafood at onshore facilities.

DID YOU KNOW?
There is worldwide disapproval of the fact that Norway allows whaling. Much of the whale meat is exported to Japan, where the price paid for it is much higher than in Norway.

▶ Fishing is central to the way of life of many coastal communities, with numerous small fishing villages scattered along the coast of Norway.

Although the number of people working in Norway's fishing industry declined during the late twentieth century, the annual catch increased, owing to improved working methods and new technology and equipment. Norway is one of the largest seafood producers in the world and the second-largest exporter of seafood and fish products after China.

Hydroelectric power and other industries

Norway has enormous hydroelectric potential because about one-fifth of the country is over 900 m (2,950 feet) above sea level, and half of Norway's 65,000 largest lakes are located at heights of over 500 m (1,650 feet).

The success of industrial development in Norway has largely been based on this inexpensive hydroelectric power. Producing metals, such as aluminium, copper, nickel and zinc, uses large amounts of electric power, as does the manufacture of fertilisers and explosives. Pulp and paper manufacture also uses a lot of electricity as well as wood from the country's forests.

⬤ Norwegian industry is built on the plentiful supply of inexpensive hydroelectric power, produced by numerous power plants, such as this power plant at Gudbrandsdal, eastern Norway.

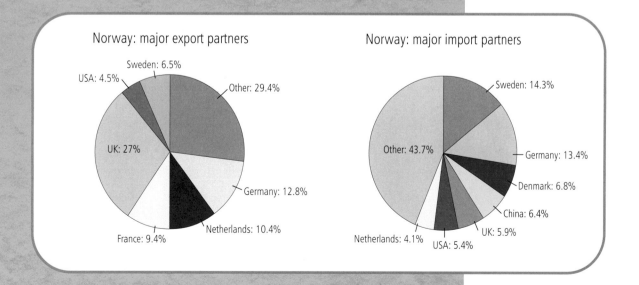

Norway: major export partners

Sweden: 6.5%
USA: 4.5%
Other: 29.4%
UK: 27%
Germany: 12.8%
France: 9.4%
Netherlands: 10.4%

Norway: major import partners

Sweden: 14.3%
Other: 43.7%
Germany: 13.4%
Denmark: 6.8%
China: 6.4%
UK: 5.9%
USA: 5.4%
Netherlands: 4.1%

Farming and food

The mountainous landscape, poor, thin soil and cold climate make farming difficult in Norway. Nevertheless, there are small farms scattered throughout the country, even though farmland only covers 3 per cent of the land.

A fertile area

The area around Oslo fjord is fairly flat. Here the land is intensely cultivated because of its rich soil, plentiful rainfall during the growing season, high summer temperatures and large markets nearby.

Western Norway has some livestock and dairy farming, and the sheltered inland fjord areas of Hardanger have some fruit-growing areas that specialise in apples and cherries. Meat and dairy production is sufficient for the country's needs, but most fruit and vegetables are imported.

Forest management

Forestry provides a second source of income for many farmers, and forests cover around 30 per cent of the Norwegian mainland. All forests are managed. Some trees are harvested for the wood-processing, pulp and paper industries. Other forests are managed for recreational use and some are protected.

⬤ Goats, with their ability to thrive in mountainous areas, are found throughout Norway, and are kept for both milk and meat.

Facts at a glance

Farmland:
3% of total land area

Main agricultural exports:
cheese, soya bean oil, prepared foods, animal skins and fur

Main agricultural imports:
prepared food, wine, pastry, chocolate

Average daily calorie intake:
3,460

A simple diet

Norwegian food is linked to the natural ingredients available. Fish dishes such as salmon, cod and mackerel are popular. Milk products, especially cheese, are also important. *Brunost* (which literally means 'brown cheese'), a sweet, semi-hard cheese, is eaten thinly sliced on bread for breakfast. Other traditional foods include sour-cream porridge, mutton, boiled shrimp, and dishes based on meat from reindeer, moose or elk. Norwegian fruits and berries, such as cloudberries and loganberries, are served for dessert.

In recent times, Norwegian eating habits have, as in the rest of the world, become international. Fast foods, such as pizza and hamburgers, are popular, and Chinese, Indian and Italian dishes are available throughout the country.

DID YOU KNOW?

Norwegian cheese is mainly eaten as thin slices. The cheese slicer (*ostehøvel*) was invented by Bjørklund, a Norwegian carpenter, in 1925. The word *høvel* in Norwegian means 'plane', a carpenter's tool.

▼ Fish is an important part of the Norwegian diet and is sold daily, fresh from the sea. Salmon, cod and mackerel, shellfish, crab, caviar, and many other types of fish can be bought, either fresh or prepared, from fish markets throughout Norway.

Transport and communications

The mountains, fjords, climate and vast distances make travelling throughout Norway difficult, and the building of roads and railways challenging. Ferries link islands to the mainland, and travel between north and south is mainly by aeroplane. In recent years, road and rail networks have been improved, using income from the oil industry.

Facts at a glance

Total roads: 92,946 km (57,754 miles)
Paved roads: 72,033 km (44,759 miles)
Major airports: 13
Major ports: 8

Roads, tunnels and bridges

Road conditions vary greatly, depending on location, weather and time of year. Major routes follow the valleys or the coasts. Mountain roads are narrow and winding, with many tunnels, and are often closed due to snow in winter. The Sognefjell Road, in the Jotunheimen Mountains, is the highest mountain pass in Northern Europe. This mountain road runs from the Sognefjord (the world's second-longest fjord), past Galdhøpiggen (Norway's highest mountain) and Jostedalsbreen (mainland Norway's largest glacier), to Gudbrandsdalen.

The *Trollstigen* ('Trolls' Path') has an incredible 11 hairpin bends. According to folklore, trolls roam the mountains at night but turn to stone when hit by sunlight each morning.

DID YOU KNOW? The Lærdal Tunnel is the world's longest road tunnel. To reduce claustrophobia, the tunnel has three large mountain caves with blue or green lighting, where drivers can take a short rest.

As technology improves, new bridges tend to be bigger, better and more spectacular than earlier versions. The Hardanger Bridge, which opened in 2013 to replace the ferry across Hardangerfjord,is 1,380 m (4,530 feet). This is 100 m (328 feet) longer than the Golden Gate Bridge in San Francisco.

The Atlantic Road, in the western fjords, connects small islands and fishing villages. The road zigzags across low bridges, which jut out over the sea. Travelling along this 8.72 km (5.5 mile) stretch is incredibly spectacular during storms. In calmer weather, whales and seals can be spotted.

The Eiksund Tunnel, on the north-west coast of Norway, is the deepest under-the-sea road tunnel in the world. Opened in 2008, the tunnel connects mainland Norway and Hareidlandet island.

⬤ The 20-km (12-mile) long Flam Railway, surrounded by steep mountains, roaring waterfalls and deep valleys, is one of the world's steepest railway lines.

Communications today

Most Norwegians have a mobile phone. Internet use is also very high, with nine out of ten Norwegians below the age of 55 using the Internet on a daily basis. Keeping in touch through emails and webcams, shopping, banking and playing games online have become important aspects of life in Norway.

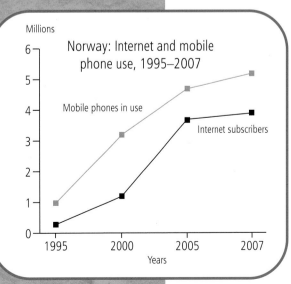

Norway: Internet and mobile phone use, 1995–2007

Millions

Mobile phones in use

Internet subscribers

Leisure and tourism

Most Norwegians enjoy the outdoors. Hiking in the forests and mountains is very popular, both with Norwegians and tourists. Some hikers carry their own tents, while others stay in hostels, or ramble from cabin to cabin. Norway is well known for its picturesque mountains, fjord-indented coastline, waterfalls, lakes and woods.

Facts at a glance
Tourist arrivals (millions)
1995   2.88
2000   3.1
2005   3.82
2008   4.44
2011   4.96

Skiing and the Winter Olympics

No one really knows who invented skiing. Rock paintings found in Bøla, Norway, dating from about 4,000 BCE, show a man on skis and, according to Norse folklore, skiing was invented by Skadi, the snowshoe goddess.

◀ Cruising is a popular tourist activity in Norway. This cruise ship is at the end of the famous Geiranger fjord.

Modern skiing developed in 1850, when a Norwegian, Sondre Norheim, invented the equipment and techniques that led to the skiing we know today. He is known as 'the father of skiing'.

For many years, Norway has been famous for its excellent cross-country skiing terrain and facilities. More recently, top-quality alpine skiing facilities have been developed, and ski resorts have expanded their accommodation to cater for the many tourists attracted by Norway's ideal snow conditions and climate.

▲ Lillehammer, Norway's oldest winter sports centre, offers great skiing with access to numerous individual pistes and many kilometres of downhill skiing, as well as wonderful scenery.

Norway has hosted the Olympic Winter Games twice, in Oslo in 1952 and in Lillehammer in 1994. This has helped tourism in Norway, showing the great winter sports facilities to the world.

Other leisure activities

Other commonly played sports include football, handball and athletics. The world's largest football tournament for young players aged 10 to 18, the Norway Cup, is held annually in Oslo and attracts teams from over 30 countries.

Climbing is also popular. Trollveggen is Europe's highest vertical rock face and a challenge for even the most experienced climber. In addition to sports clubs, many Norwegian children are members of scouts and guides, folk dance groups, environmental organisations, musical groups and choirs.

DID YOU KNOW? The Norwegian writer Henrik Ibsen (1828–1906) is often referred to as 'the father of modern drama'. He is the most frequently performed playwright in the world after Shakespeare.

Environment and wildlife

Norway's large latitudinal range, its varied landscape, altitude, soil and climate, provide a wide variety of wildlife habitats. The mountains are home to reindeer and polar fox, and the forests to elk, deer and lynx. Minke whales and seals are found off the coast. There are many species of mammals, fish and plants which are endangered and so protected.

Safeguarding Norway's natural environments

Over the past 100 years, Norway's urban areas have grown and its wilderness areas have been greatly reduced. However, Norwegians are determined to preserve their natural environment, as shown by the 25 national parks they have established on mainland Norway.

Many Norwegian children are members of a nationwide club called 'Inky Arms and his Eco-Detectives'. The children actively work in their local communities, encouraging their parents to buy sustainable goods and to recycle waste.

▶ A polar bear, the world's largest land carnivore, moves across the snowy wastes of the Norwegian Arctic wilderness. Norway is one of only five nations with polar bears.

Acid rain

Forests and waterways have been polluted by Norway's own industries and by airborne pollution from Central Europe and the British Isles. Acid rain has caused the loss of many fish, aquatic animals and plants. Since 1980, the amount of acid rain has roughly halved, but it is taking many years to repair the damage to aquatic flora and fauna.

Svalbard

Svalbard, a group of islands located at the edge of the polar ice cap, nearly 1,000 km (600 miles) north of mainland Norway, is the northernmost part of the Kingdom of Norway. The islands are Arctic wilderness areas, very mountainous and largely covered with ice. This environment is extremely vulnerable to human activities, so tourism is restricted. Nearly 60 per cent of Svalbard is protected wilderness area, with six national parks, where polar bears and reindeer roam freely and walruses flourish off the coast.

DID YOU KNOW?
The Svalbard Global Seed Vault, located inside a remote frozen mountain, was built to protect the world's plant diversity. Seeds from 526,000 different crops are stored here.

The harsh environment of the Dovrefjell mountain area inspired Edvard Grieg to compose the music 'In the Hall of the Mountain King' for Henrik Ibsen's play *Peer Gynt*.

Glossary

acid rain rain polluted with industry-produced acids

archipelago chain of islands

Arctic Circle invisible circle of latitude on the Earth's surface at 66°33' north

aurora borealis displays of light and colour in the winter skies, caused when sun particles come into contact with the upper atmosphere

compulsory something that must be done

confirmation Christian ceremony when a person confirms the promises made on their behalf at baptism

culture way of life and traditions of a particular group of people

export good or service that is sold to another country

fjord long, narrow, steep-sided coastal valley, cut into the land by glaciers and then flooded by the sea

GDP total annual value of goods and services produced by a country, measured over a year

glacier large, slow-moving river of ice, formed by many layers of compacted snow

habitat natural home of a plant or animal

hydroelectric power electricity made using the power of water

Ice Age very cold period when ice sheets cover the land

import good or service that is bought from another country

indigenous people group of people with the earliest historical connection to the land where they live

intensely cultivated producing the highest amount of crops possible

kindergarten pre-school education for young children

latitude how far north or south a place is from the Equator

latitudinal range extent that a country covers from south to north

life expectancy average period that a person may be expected to live

natural resources water, soil, vegetation and minerals that are found naturally in an area

North Atlantic Drift northern extension of the Gulf Stream in the northern Atlantic Ocean, which affects the climate of north-west Europe

plateau wide area of flat land high up in hills and mountains

precipitation any moisture that falls to the ground, including rain, snow, sleet and hail

revenue income; money

rural to do with the countryside or agriculture

Scandinavia a region in northern Europe that extends to the north of the Arctic Circle and includes Denmark, Norway and Sweden

sparsely thinly, not densely

sustainable goods products whose manufacturing, purchase and use allow for economic development while still conserving resources

United Nations some nations working together for peace and development, based on the principles of justice, human dignity and well-being

United Nations Human Development Index way of measuring standard of living, based on national income, education, health and life expectancy

urban to do with towns/cities and town/city life

welfare system programme that offers care for the sick, the elderly and disabled, and the unemployed

wilderness area undisturbed, wild, natural environment

Topic web

Use this topic web to explore Norwegian themes in different areas of your curriculum.

Science
Find out why, in areas north of the Arctic Circle, during summer the sun never completely sets and during winter these areas experience a long polar night. Draw and label diagrams to show the movement of the Earth around the sun in summer and winter.

History
Find out about the Vikings, their way of life and their travels, discoveries and conquests.

Geography
Make a crossword puzzle that contains geographical words relating to the physical landscape of Norway (e.g. mountain, fjord, glacier, waterfall).

ICT
Prepare a presentation of images to show different types of leisure activities (e.g. skiing, hiking, mountaineering, etc.) that are popular with both Norwegians and tourists.

Norway

Maths
Find out how many Norwegian krone (NOK) there are in £1. Select food for a picnic in the Norwegian countryside, then work out how much each item in the picnic would cost in NOK.

Citizenship
Using the Internet, find out more about 'Inky Arms and his Eco-Detectives'. Draw cartoons of the activities children are involved in to help safeguard the environment for future generations.

Music
Listen to 'In the Hall of the Mountain King' by Edvard Grieg. Find out about Edvard Grieg's life and how the beauty of Norway's landscape, rivers, brooks, mountains and woodlands influenced his music.

English
Using reference books, tourist brochures, the Internet and other sources of information, plan and write a programme for an exciting 10-day holiday to Norway for your family.

Further information and index

Further reading

Barnaby Bear goes to Norway (Big Book), Elaine Jackson (The Geographical Association, 2003)
The Warrior Troll, Rachael Lindsay (Nightingale Books, 2007)
Viking Life (Invasion and Settlement, Homes, Clothes, Transport), Nicola Barber (Wayland, 2010)

Web

http://news.bbc.co.uk/1/hi/world/europe/country_profiles/1023276.stm
Background information, current news and a timeline of major events in Norwegian history
www.kidskonnect.com/subject-index/26-countriesplaces/326-norway.html
Information and facts about Norway, including links to other websites
www.bbc.co.uk/learningzone/clips/bear.barnaby
BBC Learning Zone Broadband Class Clips: Barnaby Bear visits Norway

Index